EVERYONE'S GUIDE TO INVESTING

AUTHOR: Kathleen Boston McCune

Copyright 2024 by Kathleen Boston McCune

All rights reserved. No part of this book may be reproduced, stored in a retrieval system or transmitted in any form or by any means without the prior written permission of the publisher, except by a reviewer who may quote brief passages in a review to be printed in a newspaper, magazine or journal.

First printing

Referenced material is at back of book.

Photo used in cover art and within book have been created by author.

Printed in the United States of America

Other Books

By

Kathleen Boston McCune

Susanna Fuller White Winslow, My 10th Great Grandmother

Pioneers With Purpose

Mayflower Voyage,

An Historical Treatise

Memories of a Baby Boomer

Living Life Fully

Dating in Our World

And Novels:

Assignment ~ Love

Assignment ~ NOLA

Assignment ~ Cote d'Azur

Assignment ~ Texas Border

Preamble

Knowing I could invest well has been a thorn in my side most of my life. The real problem was that I never had an extra two dollars to actually invest, let alone the minimum of at least $1,000.00 when 14 and learning of this hidden talent[1].

Having a natural talent for something for which one has no money is a feeling most of us all have at one time or another, so I know most of you who are reading this missive, fully understand.

Flash forward sixty years and I am suddenly a widow. My husband had physical problems typical of an 81 year old man, but most of us think our partners and even ourselves will live forever.

After his death to pneumonia just prior to the pandemic of Covid, I realized my entire life had just changed. I would have to sell our home, as my social security

---

[1] See Chapter One

and contract positions was not enough to maintain any home.

Asking a friend who had her own Real Estate Agency to sell our home, I soon found that its' value had doubled in the ten years we lived in it and improved/maintained all usual aspects of decent property.

Most importantly, I realized that for the first time in my life I would have enough money to invest!

Once the final sale was completed. I decided I wanted to do this investing myself and chose E*TRADE for my medium.

It was easier than one might imagine and thus, I want to share with all widows, widowers and others who don't feel they could possibly invest their own money with a positive result to never say never!

CONTENTS

PAGE	TOPIC
3	Authors other books
5	Preamble
6	Contents
7	Chapter One, Business Class
22	Chapter Two, Keeping Touch
32	Chapter Three, Brokerages
37	Chapter Four, Bear Market
48	Chapter Five, Bull Market
60	Chapter Six, Losses
62	Chptr Seven, Insider Trading
67	Chptr Eight, Timing is Everything
72	Author, Credits

CHAPTER ONE ~
BUSINESS CLASS AT AGE 14

Enjoying every type of challenge in school, and running out of choices in my last year of junior high school, had me considering Personal Investing, which was a course offered for anyone planning on college, where a career earning additional monies should require investment.

When I signed up for the class, I found most of my fellow classmates were also those taking pre-college course work with me and that most of them, other than I, would have real money with which to invest.

I asked our teacher how this would work for me, since I had only baby sitting money and a wee bit for birthdays, etc.

She assured me it could still be done as far as finding the results of our efforts, however; unlike the classmates with actual money, I would only have the on-paper results, and nothing additional in my bank account.

I was still gung-ho to find out if this field would be as much fun as I had always imagined, so went ahead and then we pulled together our portfolios.

My choices included those investments considered strong and sure, such as IBM, General Motors and GE; which I noted were also in the portfolios of my classmates whose Dads worked in one of the local banks or ran one of the major Silo storage facilities for wheat, etc. for our farming community.

So far, so good, I figured. Determining what to fill in the gaps for potential gain was the more elusive, but also the greater fun (for me) because it would or could make or break the rest of the investments.

Sooooo, knowing how smart my father was, I enlisted his help by admitting what I was doing, though I didn't tell him about my friends having real money in their portfolios. His own job as a Realtor had recently been eliminated in St. Louis due to several large manufacturing firms closing which eliminated two new subdivisions for which he was the main Realtor and for which he had depended upon for our income.

Dad recommended the conglomerates, explaining how they pretty much had a monopoly in their field, and thus would do well as long as they were allowed to remain so large. Thus his recommendations included AT&T, EXXON Mobil (Standard Oil at that time) and Boeing, then in Wichita, Kansas. The first two because of their buying up much of their competition, but Boeing because they were integral in the manufacture of the planes for the military.

This was the full extent of my choices for investments, except for the newest venture of futures in the crops growing around us!

We made a chart on which we kept track of our investments, adding the results daily, taken from the *Salina Journal*'s Stock Market in the Business Section of the paper.

Over that Semester of 4 months, which ended the last day of December, my investments grew from a pretend $700.00 to $928.24. That was a 32.61% gain overall; not bad for an era when politics was so contentious and the sitting President Kennedy essentially furthering a cold war with Russia with the Bay of Pigs in Cuba on April 17, 1961.

Kathleen McCune   Guide to Investing

1960 Companies Invested in	Profits	Assets		1961 Companies Invested in	Profits	Assets	growth	Actual +--
Current View: 1-100	($ millions)	($ millions)			($ millions)	($ millions)		
General Motors	11,233.10	873.1	1	**General Motors**	12,736.00	959	1,502.90	113.3792
Exxon Mobil	7,910.70	629.8	2	**Exxon Mobil**	8,034.70	688.6	124.00	101.5675
Ford Motor	5,356.90	451.4	3	Ford Motor	5,237.90	427.9		
General Electric	4,349.50	280.2	4	**General Electric**	4,197.50	200.1	-152.00	96.50535
U.S. Steel	3,643.00	254.6	5	U.S. Steel	3,698.50	304.2		
Mobil	3,092.90	164	6	Mobil	3,178.10	182.6		
Gulf Oil	2,713.00	290.5	7	Chrysler	3,007.00	32.2		
Texaco	2,678.00	354.3	8	Texaco	2,980.30	391.8		
Chrysler	2,643.00	-5.4	9	Gulf Oil	2,720.80	330.3		
Esmark	2,475.50	19.1	10	**AT&T Technologies**	2,640.40	124.5	325.50	106.6613
AT&T Technologies	2,314.90	102.2	11	Esmark	2,442.50	18.4		
DuPont	2,114.30	418.7	12	Bethlehem Steel	2,178.10	121.2		
Bethlehem Steel	2,055.70	117.2	13	DuPont	2,142.60	381.4		
Amoco	1,956.80	139.6	14	Amoco	2,005.80	144.8		
CBS	1,910.70	85.9	15	**General Dynamics**	1,987.70	-27.1	175.80	109.7025
Armour	1,869.80	14.1	16	CBS	1,955.70	79.1		
General Dynamics	1,811.90	31.1	17	Shell Oil	1,827.80	144.6		
Shell Oil	1,810.00	147.4	18	Armour	1,735.60	16.2		
Boeing	1,612.20	12.4	19	Navistar International	1,683.30	53.7		
Kraft	1,605.70	49.4	20	Kraft	1,667.20	50.7		
Goodyear Tire & Rubber	1,579.30	76	21	ChevronTexaco	1,663.40	266.1		
ChevronTexaco	1,564.80	253.6	22	**Boeing**	1,554.60	24.5	-57.60	96.42724
Union Carbide	1,531.30	171.6	23	Goodyear Tire & Rubber	1,550.90	71	1,918.60	624.24
	29,232.30	1928.8			31,150.90	1969.6		4%

13 | Page

This chart shows the gain only on the major stocks, which only garnered a +4% for 4 mo.

To explain any increase in these stocks during a market which was technically sliding due to politics, the variance requires essentially understanding where the United States was politically, economically and technologically. This was the year that produced the first semi-conductor laser through GE and the magnetron which is integral in microwave ovens.

EXXON was known in 1960 as <u>Standard Oil</u>, which was still undercutting all competition with discounted shipping rates arranged by Rockefeller[ii].

General Motors, as always was then also known for Chevys, Pontiacs, Oldsmobiles, Buicks & Cadillacs; and in 1960 GM developed the turbo charger for V6 six cylinders) engines, terrifically popular with men, including Dad.

AT&T has always been under scrutiny as a potential or realized monopoly with both Bell Telephone and AT&T together. However, in 1960 the argument was still in the air and would remain there until 1980, thus, most folks with a telephone in their home paid money to AT&T and they were still a valid and known stock to own at that time.

General Dynamics was known to Dad because they were the first makers of the Navy's submarines. From there they eventually built the B-24 Liberators, which Daddy flew in, as a waist-gunner during WWII out of England and over Germany. Of course he was partial to this stock, as he and mother both worked for GDA while in Salina during the missile crisis. Dad explained that eventhough they lost money that year; which was due to the Federal antitrust suit and the public's lack of understanding of it, I still felt a need to honor his wishes to test their stock for my class work.

What really saved my butt though, was investing in soybean futures, which was recommended by a great uncle whose family had acquiesced to the governments offer to buy out the farmers producing food crops to keep prices down for the public, but high enough to keep those farmers from bankruptcy and in a tenable position to finish their retirement on the farm, when most of their younger family members had chosen to find their professions in the cities.

Thus, my investment of a pretend $100.00 that year for soybean futures became a $304.00 profit.

The formula to determine profit or loss is:

$$\frac{\text{Price Sold} - \text{Purchase Price}}{\text{Purchase Price}} \times 100$$

$$\frac{\$928.24 - \$700.00}{\$700.00} \times 100 = 32.6\%$$

One of the points to remember when choosing stocks is getting a good feel for how the rest of the world is reacting politically, personally and what are folks buying and why?

Boeing, like the rest of the choices I made for investing, was also the result of a conglomeration of purchases of smaller airline firms either seeking the purchase or headed in that direction prior to their purchase by William E. Boeing. His real flight (pun intended) to fame was his plane which could land on water, the B&W seaplane. In 1931 the firm merged it's 4 smaller airlines into United Airlines. Then In 1960, the company bought Vertol Aircraft Corporation, which at the time, was the biggest independent manufacturer of helicopters. This was why Dad felt Boeing should be a part of my portfolio, particularly since Boeing had been a part of Wichita, Kansas since 1928. And truthfully, until that year, they had made fantastic growth seem easy; however, they would leave Wichita in 2013, ignoring thousands of Wichitan's who wouldn't qualify to move to Seattle. In 1960 to 1961, they lost for me $3.50.

Today, April of 2024, Boeing is facing bad raps due to parts flying off their planes across the World, causing their current CEO, David Calhoun to retire at the EOY 2024. Not knowing results now or in future, I currently sold that stock, but may repurchase it if a viable CEO takes over, one who will at least return oversight on the planes to include

Supervisors and real mechanics, sooner than later! Now, sadly, I cringe and pray a lot when family members are flying anywhere!

It is for this kind of situation that requires all good investors to read the <u>Wall Street Journal</u> daily, as well as staying abreast of most everything affecting the financial world in which we live.

The most important aspect of choosing your own investments is in your attachment to them and having a viable reason to feel they will most likely make you and themselves money in the future.

Keeping track of each and every one of your choices is key to having a hold on your money. Ignoring even the most viable stock when purchased, may mean a pain in your pocket down the road.

Problems inherent in our world, such as politics and who is in charge of our lives; is key to what happens on the stock market.

CHAPTER TWO ~

KEEPING TOUCH WITH EVERY ONE OF YOUR STOCKS, WHILE KEEPING YOUR EARS AND EYES OPEN AND AWARE OF POTENTIAL FUTURE STOCK PURCHASES:

Politically, Republican Presidents usually garner a better stock position, if they also have a Republican Senate and House in DC.

The reason for this is that for most regimes, it was Republicans who spent our taxes to make progress financially for the country, not giving away money to the poor without requiring work to ensue first; thus leaving the feeding and housing of the poor to Churches and families.

To illuminate my meaning, President Johnson was the first President to use the interest earnings on our Social Security for other programs outside of what it was meant to be, which was the future of those who were enforced to take it from our earnings for future use after retirement. That date has continued to become older and older, until it nearly now reaches the same date we are expected to be buried. For men that is 76 and for women 81. When we can't draw on our SS until age 66 (currently), that only gives us ten years for men and fifteen years for women to draw what we have put into over our earning years since childhood! If our interest earnings had been left for us and attached to each of our SS earnings, we would today be realizing checks over a plus 12% at least, without the compounding of additional earnings on our SS afterwards. Depressing at the very least when one contemplates what those figures might be! For now, if you have even ten percent you can put aside after real expenses, you should do it and if you invest in stocks, you will make more overall, even if you only invest in what is called the Dividend Aristocrats (those stocks which have earned more money for over 25 consecutive years).

Those stocks and their founders:

1. Berkshire Hathaway (Warren Buffet's).
2. Amazon(Jeff Bezos)
3. Vanguard High-Dividend Yield ETF(John C Bogle)
4. Procter & Gamble(William Proctor & James Gamble)
5. McDonalds (Ray Kroc)
6. Tesla (Elon Musk, Martin Eberhard & Marc Tarpinning)
7. Starbucks (Jerry Baldwin, Gordon Bowker, Zev Siegl)
8. Apple (Steve Jobs, Steve Wozniak, Ronald Wayne)
9. Microsoft (Bill Gates & Paul Allen)
10. Sysco (Herbert Irving, Harry Rosenthal, John F. Baugh)

What seems consistent with all these founders is dedication in what they are sure is necessary to a majority of the public and an overall acumen of plying

their trades with that same dedication and surety of great results.

For you as an investor, finding the money makers is the most difficult, as one has to consider all typical reasons why they may or may not fail, thus causing their price to fall, and you losing your money.

The known ones already listed are a given, and if you read regularly of those who are upcoming, you will find that many of them are also bought as stock by Berkshire Hathaway, who is number one in earnings overall, so being "in the game" includes listening for new areas of economy via the youngsters and what we read on Facebook, "X", etc.

Some of those reasons are not always apparent, because that includes who is in charge of the firm, their CEO and what is his or her reputation from other such positions. When you invest in a firm, you get voting rights for their stock meetings and then you will want to have an idea for whom you are voting.

Key to making more money and not losing what you've already invested is keeping your ear to the ground, as the Native Americans used to say. For them it secured their lives. For investors it secures your income as far as that which is in the stock market.

Choose your stock based upon your areas of knowledge, whether that is your daily Starbucks, clothing (Christian Dior; Levi;

Victoria's Secret, etc. Or shoes: Tod's; Prada, etc. Or Louis Vuitton, Gucci, LVMH, etc.).

Your stock should be of what you do every day of your life, and thus be those areas of daily concern to you which your ear is naturally turned to for your own sense of security even before putting money into those providers of coffee (Starbucks).

Whatever you decide upon, start actually listening to your fellow staff wherever you work, or if you aren't hybrid and at an office, watch the ads for shows you watch on TV. If you are watching them, others with your interests are also watching them and the ads will follow everyone's interests, assuming the producers of the shows are marketing their ads before allowing them to follow those shows.

Also, be aware of the World around you. That means even outside of the US, which in today's world, truly means the entire universe. As a matter of fact, about 90% of the goods coming into America are made in other countries, most notably, China.

Though most Americans would prefer to purchase goods made in America, to support our own folks, China's wages paid to those laborers making our goods are around 30 percent of what is paid to manufacturing laborers in America. Which today (April 2024) is around $15.88 hr. in American vs $4.81 in China.

Thus, the reduced price of those goods and the resulting markets which sell them, only increase the orders with such a return, which includes most owners who are Americans, and most particularly Walmart. I remember their father (current owners father) bragging about Walmart selling as many American made products as he could find, but his kids never made that pledge and I feel sure have no plans to change in the near future.

Whether you feel comfortable investing in the firms who don't support America except to get every last penny for their goods, or not, do remember that the "Mom & Pop" businesses were what made America in the first place.

CHAPTER THREE ~

CHOOSING YOUR BROKERAGE FIRM

The amount of time on your hands will determine whether or not you hire your own Investor at a brokerage firm privately or venture into the field yourself through at least what I consider in alpha-order the top ten Investment Houses for online and independent investors.

Remember that you will be doing all the work, not just saying what general avenue of investments you think is a good idea, but actually inputting your investment or (bet) as several of my Professors termed the stock market and those enterprises.

However, the rewards will also be yours alone as will those choices which fail for many reasons; all of which you will eventually see and at least learn their reasons for why; though it is usually many more reasons than are published.

ONLINE BROKERAGE HOUSES

NAME	FEES	Minimum Acct Rqrd	PROMOTION?	RATING
ALLYInterest	0	$0	$100 - $3000 with qualifying deposit	4.5%
AMERITRADE (TD)	0	$0	NONE	5.0%
CHARLES SCHWAB	0	$0	NONE	5.0%
E*TRADE from Morgan Stanley	0	$0	$600 with new acct	4.5%
FIDELITY	0	$0	$100 with new acct	5.0%
INTERACTIVE	0	$0	NONE	5.0%
MERRILL EDGE	0	$0	$600 with new acct	4.5%
TRADE STATION	0	$500	$150 with 1st $500 dep	4.5%
WE BULL	0	$0	NONE	4.5%
ZACKSTRADE	$0.01 per share	$2,500	NONE	4.0%

Choosing the ONE for you is clearly up to you, the investor. By writing out what you have to invest, what you plan on investing in and what parameters you expect to earn may be described in one of the top ten recommended brokerage houses above.

Personally, I chose E*TRADE (now with Morgan Stanley) and have been happy with my results which reflect my choices of investments, coupled with their quickness of making it happen. Of course the stocks I have invested in will have the same results, no matter which Brokerage House one chooses, but ask friends, family and fellow staff who they use before deciding on the ONE for your investments.

CHAPTER FOUR ~

CHOOSING YOUR STOCK IN A BEAR MARKET

iii

Definition: Bear Markets are when a market experiences prolonged price declines. This typically is a percentage change downward of 20% over at least a 2- month period. It is exacerbated when the owners of those stocks internalize the decline and make foolish decisions which means, selling too many stocks short (or selling stocks which the investor feels will decline in value in the future).

When I first began writing this guide the market was considered to be a Bear Market (from January 2022 to October 2022), but this was truly individually for me and those who have asked my opinion and followed it, inaccurate. You see, we were not under even 5% of our original investment, and thus not even close to the general investing public who have for whatever reason chosen stocks which have not engendered the faith of the majority of those holding those stocks who have sold them short, or at least believe their stocks weren't worth holding onto and have added to what appears to be a bear market.

Thus, avoiding a bear market is actually possible if choosing one's stock with an attitude based more on value from knowledge and data than popularity of others' choices.

I personally feel that Bear Markets are the result of newer investors believing what is told them by the public news organizations seeking new viewers and the Federal Reserve and their stock brokers who have not their best interests in mind for stock, but only the interest charges on bonds, new business loans and real estate.

Of course the Pandemic of Covid during the last Bear Markets actually coerced that one, which lasted ten months, from January 2022 until October of 2022. Whomever was responsible for so heinous, demoralizing and devastating as was the Covid virus should rot in Hell the next lifetime they pull, however; the result on the stock market was inevitable.

Know yourself and follow the precepts of what have brought you the funds you now have to invest which is of course, logic, studying potential future worth, consideration of true value in the long haul for those intelligent and diligent enough to actually own stocks and businesses which are growing with the future, but still have a hand on the past which is necessary in the real world.

For instance, buy stocks which are seeking lithium and copper for future batteries of electrically run vehicles in the penny stock, but also have a larger share of Shell or Exxon to ride the larger and more sure wave of gasoline fueled vehicles for now and the next ten years (unless the current tides change sooner than that).

Find a friend (or ask your little brother or IT brained Uncle) which of the x-box stocks he invests in and what he foresees in the future.

Some of my most lucrative stock has come from keeping my ear to ground when young male relatives or fellow staff are chatting up what they see as a good buy, if they just had the money to invest!

Also, invest in your pleasures, be it camping, gambling, shooting at the range, or movies. All have their own stock. Camping includes: Vista Outdoor, Inc (VSTO); Shooting has: (SWBI), or Smith and Wesson; and the movies have: Cinemark Holdings or (CNK), (AMC) and (IMAX), while gambling has: (MGM), (CZR), (WYNN), (BALY) & (CHDN) or Churchill Downs for the horsey set.

None of these are that expensive and how much more fun to check out your own passions daily!

Historically, things like precious metals, consumer staples, commodities, utilities, health care, and transportation stocks perform well in a bear market. Even the experts say these stocks are positioned well - even in a down market.

As stated by: Sujai Shivakumar, Charles Wessner[iv] and Thomas Howell:[v]

"An initial assessment of recent attempts by the United States to limit or delay China's ability to acquire and produce advanced semiconductor technologies reveals a mixed picture in a complex and rapidly evolving industry. On the one hand, new chip restrictions have significantly affected China's semiconductor ecosystem, limiting access to equipment essential for next-generation production. On the other hand, China is intensifying its domestic investments in more advanced chips while also reducing market shares of U.S. firms—and by extension, the revenues U.S. firms need to invest in the next-generation of technology. Over time, this loss of market share could well undermine the competitiveness of U.S. firms in this key industry. The initial volley of restrictions has also revealed limitations of export controls, both because the technology is rapidly changing and because there are gaps in compliance between U.S. companies and those of allies.

One key conclusion, however, is that there is "no way back" to the global semiconductor ecosystem that existed prior to the pandemic. The U.S. chip supply chain vulnerabilities that the Covid-19 emergency exposed are too alarming to allow a reversion to a business-as-usual supply chain anchored in China. Further, Chinese perceptions of the United States' reliability as a supplier have understandably changed. It is unlikely that U.S.-China semiconductor-related trade will return to the *status quo ante*.

While the United States retains a substantial lead in semiconductor design and certain equipment, the most advanced chips are no longer manufactured by U.S.-based firms. This has troubling implications for new technologies such as artificial intelligence (AI) and quantum as well as for the security of supply for key industrial inputs. The administration is to be commended for recognizing the central importance of the industry, its vulnerabilities, and the fact that the industry has been both challenged abroad and neglected at home. As the world enters a period of renewed policy focus on this enabling technology, it is important that the government's analytic capabilities are improved to inform policy, develop effective mechanisms for allied coordination, and create the government-industry partnerships and long-term investments that will be needed to sustain and grow a more resilient U.S. semiconductor ecosystem."

Best and alternative stocks to buy during a Bear Market are Government Bonds and those stocks covering necessary items to the public, such as utilities and your own municipality (assuming it is being run by folks knowledgeable to govern during such crises).

Also, good bets are in food, healthcare, communications and security.

CHAPTER FIVE~~

CHOOSING YOUR STOCK IN A BULL MARKET

vi

We are currently in a Bull Market, which began October 2022 and continues thus far, including a +35% increase in stocks overall since that date. My personal investments today (April 6, 2024) are at +89.26% of my original investment in them, though the average investor's profile shows +10%.

This is the reason I decided to write this petite manual for women and/or men who are not familiar with investing in the stock market.

Generally, a Bull Market is described as a Market which grows a +20% and remains at least that high over a prolonged period of time.

We have all heard in school how dangerous it can be to put our money into the stock market since primary school, as 1929 still looms in the minds of those whose family's wealth or lack thereof was changed so drastically during that period of time in America.

The following reasons are considered to be the main culprits of the stock market crash of 1929: (overinflated shares, growing bank loans, agricultural overproduction, panic selling, stocks purchased on margin, higher interest rates, and a negative media industry).

Many of these causes have been turned around since then, with a final correction to the Market as of 1954.

Today, banks do not put themselves and their investors in positions to have this happen, as we are all aware when owning bonds or any type of platform offered by banks, that their percent of gain is only 1% or 2% in the best of a Bull Market.

Also, the government stepped into the Agriculture markets and began offering to the individual farmers money to not plant, to keep the price of goods appropriate for a healthy investing market, while insuring the foods the public enjoy are available in the quantities necessary for that to happen, while not flooding the market with foods of the same kind, dropping their prices below where the farmer can earn enough to stay in the industry.

Sadly, panic selling still is prolific in today's market by the youngsters and oldsters who truly don't understand what is going on when the Federal Reserve Bank mentions they might increase the interest rates for loans to businesses and potential home owners. The Feds do this to get a feel for how the public feels about this, as well as mentioning it just before the quarterly job market profiles are released by the government.

The result is what happened last Thursday, April 4th, 2024, when the market dipped nearly 4% when the Fed. Reserve Bank did what I just mentioned, but on Friday, April 5th, 2024, the government announced jobs were nearly 30% above the estimate being used by the Feds for their predictions, and thankfully at least half who had sold stock on Thursday, bought it back on Friday, when the Feds said "Well, maybe we won't have to consider an inflation landscape after all!" Poetic, though irritating, it at least let investors know pretty much that life

could continue at the Bullish pattern we are now enjoying.

The firm with which I invest, Morgan Stanley, say of the current market:

1. "Stay Cautious on U.S. Equities

    We continue to see risks in U.S. stocks, particularly in the market-cap-weighted benchmark indices, such as:

    - extreme concentration, with the biggest tech names weighing heavily in major indices;
    - high prices relative to potential earnings; and
    - ambitious earnings estimates pegging 2024 profits growth at 10%.

What's more, the U.S. stock market begins the year in a precarious place—overbought, with very low volatility suggesting a sense of complacency among investors.

Given such risks, we expect the S&P 500 to trade between 4,100 and 5,100 throughout the year, likely ending 2024 around 4,500.

For investors who want passive exposure to U.S. stocks, rather than actively choosing individual equities, consider investing in an equal-weighted S&P 500 strategy, which seeks to allocate equal amounts of capital to each of the 500 stocks in the index. This looks like a less risky approach than the traditional cap-weighted version, in which stocks with larger market caps represent a larger share of the index, since a substantial drop in any of the large tech stocks currently dominating the index would have a greater impact on the index as a whole.

2. Shift to Fixed Income

Consider putting a larger share of your portfolio in bonds. As interest rates remain higher for longer, investors may get better risk-adjusted returns from the annual rate paid on bonds, while potentially earning capital gains in bonds if interest rates decline in 2024, as forecast, and bond prices increase in tandem. (Bond prices typically rise when rates fall.)

In contrast to stocks, we believe U.S. Treasury bonds are closer to being fairly priced and see the 10-year yield likely ending 2024 somewhere around 3.95%, not far below its current level.

Municipal bonds and investment-grade corporate credit, paired with short-duration Treasuries, remain decent options.

3. Seek Opportunity Beyond U.S. Stocks and Bonds

Outside the U.S., we prefer investment opportunities in Japan, based on improving economic growth and inflation dynamics, as well as the yen's cheapness relative to other major currencies. We also continue to look for stock-specific opportunities in Europe, and broader index-level opportunities in select emerging markets like India, Brazil and Mexico.

Among alternative assets, we're focused on hedge funds whose managers are good stock-pickers and can use leverage and risk management to help amplify returns. Investors may also want to consider selectively investing in infrastructure, commodities such as gold and residential real estate.

Uncertainty Lingers

As always, the broader economic backdrop informs the Global Investment Committee's outlook. The year has started with accommodative financial conditions, meaning that there has generally been enough cash in the financial system for businesses and households to borrow if needed. This level of liquidity was arguably the single biggest surprise of 2023, given how aggressively the U.S. Federal Reserve hiked rates. <u>Such loose conditions are poised to reverse</u>, however, with the Fed's program of propping up regional banks expiring, plus a likely ramping up of U.S. Treasury borrowing, among other factors that could substantially drain liquidity in the financial system. This could remove a key support for today's stock valuations while helping keep rates higher for longer.

Ultimately, we're entering a year of lingering uncertainty. Inflation remains, despite the market's hope that the fight to tame it is already won. Government deficits—now running at about 7% of GDP and rapidly adding to a record debt pile of $34 trillion—may not be sustainable. And importantly, the question of where interest rates will end up for the long term hasn't yet been answered. As the year unfolds, we recommend investors stay patient and focus on the long term. As always, keep in touch with your Financial Advisor to help you position your portfolio for the risks and opportunities.

This article is based on Lisa Shalett's Global Investment Committee Weekly report from January 22, 2024, "2024 Outlook Summary: Turn, Turn, Turn." Ask your Morgan Stanley Financial Advisor for a copy. Listen to the <u>audiocast</u> based on this report.[vii]

CHAPTER SIX~~~

REMEMBER, LEAVING YOUR SAVINGS UNINVESTED IS A LOSS FROM THE BEGINNING.

When I finally had enough earnings and savings available to invest in the stock market I realized I was one of the few of business owners who hadn't already begun to do this years ago. It was with this laurel of commonality resulting in not a frugal life style, but one that included thought, which helped me feel before I realized I was good at this endeavor, and pushed me forward more quickly than even I imagined, that I would embrace the stock market.

What excitement when an unknown stock to you actually becomes a major endeavor in our economy. Such was the result of NVDA, or Nvidia. I invested in this stock five years ago for $101.94 and now it is priced at $808.08. This was one which a fellow staffer recommended and thank the Lord he did.

Remember, those friends with interests outside your own are crucial for understanding all stocks available.

Keep your ear to the potential stock seemingly forming up while we go about our daily routines. Reading Wallstreet daily and actually hearing what the children and grandchildren are discussing over and over again, may be your next potential money maker.

CHAPTER SEVEN~~~

WHAT IS INSIDER TRADING"

Be sure you follow the law as far as who is sharing what, when and where:[viii]

- An insider is someone with either access to valuable non-public information about a corporation or ownership of stock equaling more than 10% of a firm's equity.[1]
  - Insiders are legally permitted to buy and sell shares, but the transactions must be registered with the
  - SEC.[2]

U.S. Securities and Exchange Commission. "Rule 10b5-1 and Insider Trading: Proposed Rule."

- Legal insider trading happens often, such as when a CEO buys back company shares, or when employees buy stock in the company where they work.
- Illegal use of non-public material information is generally used for profit.
- The SEC monitors illegal insider trading by looking at trading volumes, which increase when there is no news released by or about the company.
- The more infamous form of insider trading is the illegal use of non-public material information for profit. It's important to remember this can be done by anyone including company executives, their friends, and relatives, or just a regular person on the street, as long as the information is not publicly known.

- For example, suppose the CEO of a publicly traded firm inadvertently discloses their company's quarterly earnings while getting a haircut. If the hairdresser takes this information and trades on it, that is considered illegal insider trading, and the SEC may take action.
- The SEC is able to monitor illegal insider trading by looking at the trading volumes of any particular stock. Volumes commonly increase after material news is issued to the public, but when no such information is provided and volumes rise dramatically, this can act as a warning flag. The SEC then investigates to determine precisely who is responsible for the unusual trading and whether or not it was illegal.

Insider Trading vs. Insider Information

- <u>Insider information</u> is knowledge of material related to a publicly-traded company that provides an unfair advantage to the trader or investor. For example, say the vice president of a technology company's engineering department overhears a meeting between the CEO and the CFO.

- Two weeks <u>before the company releases its earnings</u>, the CFO discloses to the CEO that the company did not meet its sales expectations and lost money over the past quarter. The vice president of the engineering department knows their friend owns shares of the company and warns the friend to sell their shares right away and look to open a <u>short position</u>.

This is an example of insider information because earnings have not been released to the public.

- Suppose the vice president's friend then sells their shares and shorts 1,000 shares of the stock before the earnings are released. Now it is illegal insider trading. However, if they trade the security after the earnings are released, it is not considered illegal because they do not have a direct advantage over other traders or investors.[ix]

CHAPTER EIGHT~~~

TIMING IS EVERYTHING!!!

x

For sure, though timing for our jobs, doctor's appointments, weddings, funerals, etc. have always been the KNOWN reason for timing being accurate, when one is investing in the stock market, this too is a most important aspect of actually making money. Buying timely will determine whether or not you actually own that all important stock when the rest of the World discovers it and make it a top choice for income outstanding.

Also, knowing when to sell is just as important and can make the difference of whether you are like "Kennedy during the '29 debacle" when he actually made gobs of $ selling short timely; or otherwise, you could fare as the rest of those who waited too long to get out of a situation of stock going under along with your lifetime's savings.

Though we now have the results of the government and brokerage firms cleaning up how that situation occurred, we still have "start-up" businesses that fail and ideologies by various politicians which do not always work out for the betterment of the public as a whole and their monies when invested in the wrong stock for too long or not long enough.

Stay vigilant in your daily analysis of the stock market even when on vacation or when super busy, by staying away from those stocks you feel in your gut just are scary. That is usually exactly the situation.

Consider your risk tolerances:

Before deciding on what level of portfolio risk you want to target, you will first need to assess the comfort level with risk. Will you feel frightened if the market drops more than ten or twenty percent in a month? If so, you should choose differently than those with more to lose on iffy or maybe type of stocks.

Those of you with a more conservative tolerance or availability of monies remaining, may need more in your portfolio in bonds and cash compared to stocks; or if you have a more aggressive tolerance, you will feel comfortable with a greater portion of investments in stocks.

Risk capacity considers the factors that impact your financial ability to <u>take</u> risks and should include those areas such as job status, caretaking duties, debts outstanding and how much time you have to reach that goal.

Most importantly, have fun and if investing in the stock market becomes burdensome, at least consider engaging a broker to invest for you.

And Good Luck!!

 Kathleen Boston McCune has been penning manuscripts for her heritage and for those enjoying adventure novels over the last 14 years. This self-help book on investing is for all those who, like her, want to invest, but are not sure how to start. She hopes this book will give those folks the same excitement she feels now when checking her investments daily.

[ii] By 1900 John D. Rockefeller, founder and largest shareholder of the Standard Oil Company, controlled more than 90 percent of U.S. oil production, dominating the world market.
[iii] From Shutter Stock
[iv] And Thomas Howell, Consultant

[v] https://www.csis.org/people/charles-wessner, https://www.csis.org/people/sujai-shivakumar

[vi] From Shutter Stock

[vii] https://www.morganstanley.com/ideas/are-we-in-a-bull-market-2024
[viii] **By MARY HALL Updated April 02, 2022 Reviewed by CHARLES POTTERS Fact checked by YARILET PEREZ**
[ix] **(see viii above)**
[x] **Shutterstock**

www.ingramcontent.com/pod-product-compliance
Lightning Source LLC
Chambersburg PA
CBHW070407230526
45471CB00006B/2697